Seasons

DISNEP PRESS

Los Angeles • New York

Let's name the four **seasons**.

spring

summer

fall

winter

What is **spring**?

Spring is the
time of year
when **rain** falls,

pretty **flowers**
grow,

fuzzy **chicks**
hatch,

and **Easter**
comes!

What is **summer**?
Summer is the time of year when it is hot and the days are long.

Summer is the time for sunglasses, bathing suits, and the pool!

It is the time to **surf**,

build **sandcastles**,

have a **picnic,**

and watch the **fireflies** blink at night.

What is **fall**?

Fall is the time of year when **leaves** turn many colors.

Fall is the time to pick **apples**

and bake yummy **pies**.

Fall is the time for **scarecrows**

and **pumpkins**.

Fall means it is time for **Halloween**!

What is **winter**?
Winter is the time of year
when it is **cold**.

It is the time to build **snowmen**

and throw **snowballs**!

Winter is the time
to **ice-skate**

and go **sledding**!

Christmas comes one night in winter.

And then a brand-new
year is born.
Soon it is time again
for spring!

Can you name the **season** in each scene?

winter

summer

spring

fall